THE IMAGE

THE IMAGE

A Christian Rethinks Islamic Terrorism

Handri Timbuleng

Order this book online at www.trafford.com
or email orders@trafford.com

Most Trafford titles are also available at major online book retailers.

Printed in the United States of America.

ISBN: 978-1-4669-4438-1 (sc)
ISBN: 978-1-4669-4440-4 (hc)
ISBN: 978-1-4669-4439-8 (e)

Library of Congress Control Number: 2012911324

Trafford rev. 06/27/2012

 www.trafford.com

North America & international
toll-free: 1 888 232 4444 (USA & Canada)
phone: 250 383 6864 ♦ fax: 812 355 4082

CONTENTS

ACKNOWLEDGEMENTS

I have been encouraged in the writing of this book by many people along the way, from the highest levels of our government in the United States to family, friends and colleagues. I gratefully thank The White House, which personally sent me a Christmas and New Year greeting card dated on December 5, 2011. Appreciation should also go to the family of The President of the United States of America, who gratefully responded to my personal letter. Further, I would also like to personally thank, First Lady, Mrs. Michelle Obama, for her encouragement and willingness to share my thoughts with the President regarding his leadership.

I am especially thankful for President Obama's plan that saved my house from foreclosure by lowering my interest rate. From the bottom of our heart, we as a family greatly appreciate him (through his program) for our ability to stay in our current house. God will redeem all these kindness back to the President and all of his staff. Thanks should also go to the Vice President Mr. Joe Biden, who spent his valuable time to write down and update me on the development of the country to date.

I am deeply indebted to The Presbyterian Church and all of its members, who covered all transportation and living expenses during my first years of living in the United States of America. They enabled me to be reunited with my family after several years. I believe the Lord Jesus will bless them all for all the favors they have offered us.

This book could not be completed without a consistent encouragement and feedback from Rev. David Long-Higgins, who accompanied the process of writing and editing of this book from the beginning, Dr. Y Budi Sulistioadi, PhD., also took part in editing the last portion of this book and enabled the translation of this book from the Indonesian language to English. I also thank Professor William Liddle, (major in political science of Indonesia) for his insights and ideas that helped to sharpen the academic perspective of this book. There are many others whom I cannot mention by names, but for whom I am very grateful. You are all great people I love and miss working with very much.

Letter to the President of the USA

September 20, 2011

Dear Mr. President

Herewith I would like to express my support for you. I am fully aware about how great are the challenges to be a president of this great country. Therefore, I would like to talk to you in person as we share the same faith, which is Christianity. Both of these issues are about my concerns and my hope to you.

The first concern is about the enormous financial debt of this country. I am especially concerned with the way in which this debt will become a heavy burden for our descendants (e.g. children and grand children). Hence, deeply from my heart I pray for you to decrease the amount of the national debt, and may this become your first priority in the current term, as well as in your second term.

The second concern is related to interfaith and inter-origin relationship between human being. For your information, I was born in Indonesia and I also have had a first-hand experience of the dynamic relationship between Christians and Muslims in Indonesia. As a Christian, I recognize that NOT all Muslim folks are terrorists. In fact, I am fully aware that there have been 7000 American Muslim troops who had been fought for the glory of the US in Iraq and Afghanistan.

Hence, it is my concern when people from any tradition or faith tear down the other people tradition or faith. As we learned from the movement of "Burning the Qur'an" by a Christian pastor, it was definitely not the way Christians should behave and respond to whatever had been done by our Muslim fellows. A greatly appreciate your ability to facilitate the equality of people with different faith, in taking part of the development of this great country, especially through constructive dialogue and mutual respect. It is essential for our country and for the world that such an attitude of respect had been prioritized.

Finally, I would like to offer a word of encouragement to you. May God grant you the ability to focus on the right track, even that you may have been observed the varieties of disrespectful behavior of people with one faith to fellows with different faith? Hopefully , those will not discourage you in any way. Please believe that God will grant you strength you essentially need to face this challenging phase of the leadership.

May God bless you and strengthen you beyond your own strength.

Sincerely,
Pastor Handri Timbuleng

Two Visions from God

Tuesday, August 9, 2011

Happy Birthday Mr. Barack Obama, the President of the USA. Through this letter, I would like to convey two messages from God to you:

1. No weapons that against the USA are being prospered
2. What is with you is bigger than what is against you

So, let us breakdown these two messages as follow.

The first one, God spoke to me (I believe so), you must understand that this is not all about yourself, instead, this message is widely for the whole nation that you currently lead. God Bless America. Once this nation is blessed, no one will be able to curse it. I compare this message with one story that we can find in the Old Testament of the Christian's Holy Bible. According to the relevant source in the Bible, once upon a time, an enemy wants to pay (?) the prophet, in total of two opportunities, once from each side, but it ended up with a blessing. Even the enemy finally was willing to give everything he has to the prophet.

Further, I asked to God, "Why the USA, not the other country?". In his talk, God indicates that the USA has two things related to God: (1) One Nation under God and even in the dollar bill it states "In God We Trust", then God said those are really the reasons.

The second parable, also quoted from the Christian's Holy Bible, told a story about a prophet with his servants. Once upon a time, there was a difficult situation and the servants started to scary and worry. Then asked the servants "How can you just stay calm in this situation?" since the servants realized that enormous number of soldiers came to kill them from any directions. The prophet stayed calm and said his prayer to God, and asked the servants to open their eyes. When the servants opened their eyes, in a supernatural sight, they saw the chariot angels of God equipped with the fire sword in their hands on the top of the hill. The chariot was huge, even much bigger than the number of the soldiers who came to attack them.

You may wonder why I am supporting you as a president, here are two reasons:

1. I learned that you plan to withdraw the troops from Iraq and Afghanistan, which is a brilliant idea. The following arguments support this statement: (a) War is not always the answer. It may indeed solve a particular problem in a particular area, but it definitely creates bigger problems. Just a very simple example and consideration, if we assume that one missile costs about one million dollars, and think about how many missiles had been already deployed. How much money had been the US spent for the wars over the Middle East area? And how many households will be helped

by turning this budget to recover the United States economic crisis? Or much simpler to provide food and shelter for the victim of Catharina Storm around New Orleans area? (b) While another countries in the world cut down their defense budget by up to 30% out of their total spending for their homeland security, the US keep the same amount and even much bigger portion of the defense and security spending. (c) The war just keep increasing the number of victims, who most of them are the young and potential Americans, who become idled due to the physical injury and disability. (d) Even the troops withdrawal still in progress until the year of 2014, this decision and movement essentially helps the process of recover of the US economy and especially, debt. For further illustration, total of the US debt from 1776-2004 is 3 trillion US$, which had been grown for 228 years. However, within only 7 years the debt grown rapidly up to 13 trillion, which essentially doubled by a factor of 4.

2. Me, Rev Handri Timbuleng and my colleague Rev David Long-Higgins, just edited this book, titled "The Image". The purpose of this book is really to facilitate the harmony of living between Christians, Muslim and how we should understand about terrorism. I put so much hope in this book, which is to educate people about the different perspectives, which at the end, should be able to reduce the conflict between the people of these two major religions.

Note:

For additional information, I was born in April 26, 1962 and raised in Indonesia afterwards. Indonesia is a country with the largest Muslim population (~280 millions) in the world, while the USA has 302 millions with 2 millions of them are Muslim. From this point of view, you as the current president of the USA, make us Indonesians proud, since you spent a portion of your childhood in our beloved country.

PREFACE

I wrote this book upon a request from my friend, Simeon, who has always asked me to write a book. I asked him, "What did he hope to learn?" He later told me about his interest in Islam based on the fact that I came from a country where the majority population is Muslim. Although it is not an Arab country, it is the country with the largest Muslim population of any in the world. Indonesia is the 4th largest country in the world.

I heard discussions in the aftermath of the 9/11 attacks on the World Trade Center Towers, that Indonesia became a target, of the United States Armed Forces in addition to Iraq and Afghanistan. It seemed to me that there was a need to overcome some misconceptions regarding the people of Islam.

Another reason Simeon asked me to write this booklet is I am a common person and not a professor who writes by using formulas and formulations that can sometimes be difficult to understand. Simeon also added that I have the experience of living amongst the Muslim society in Indonesia and have undergone a bitter experience that can be shared as a case study about Islam and terrorism that similarly occurred in America.

This book is a book through which the Lord warned me in many ways. The inspiration, as well as divine revelation, have become the major part of the story and even taken over the plot.

This book in many ways has become my personal repentance book, from misconceptions I have had for so long about Muslims in general. By the time I prepared this writing, I honestly was carried away by traumatic emotion from a previous experience I had when the church that I lead in Indonesia was destroyed by a Muslim group yelling, "Allah hu akbar." The Lord himself spoke to me through my memory of past events and through direct inspiration. And so the title of this book is based on this question whether Islam is a peaceful religion or a terrorist religion and what its relationship with Christianity should be.

It was my hope in writing this book that it would be both brief in length so that it could be easily accessed by many different people of various backgrounds.

This book is not a political book to support a particular president, government or religion, but rather it is my personal testimony regarding what God has made known to me. The ideas I seek to convey are so important that I hope it may come to be read and discussed by many people.

Handri Timbuleng
Columbus, OH

THE IMAGE

I must begin this book with a word about my bitter experience: It happened in the area of Bumi Serpong Damai where I lived at that time, because it was a new real estate residential area. There were not many Christians and hence not many denominations of Christians were represented. I proposed to make a fellowship for Christian people which could be accepted by many denominational groups so that we did not need to travel far to worship the LORD. The existing governmental regulations necessitated the development of a church in that area that was ecumenical in nature because there were not enough people from any one denomination to form a church on its own. Hence the Gereja Kristen Oikumene (GKO)—Ecumenical Christian Church was formed. This name means it was not attached to one denomination either in terms of the worship service style or the person who was the pastor leading any particular service. The church remained flexible, while waiting for the arrival of new people that could meet the criteria and offer the financial stability of certain denominations so that the various members of the GKO could separate themselves and stand on their own. This temporary church (GKO) served to nurture mutually good relationships amongst the various denominations. This set the stage for the future to create a harmonized relationship between the different denominations that exist. It is important to remember that humans can only provide an openness to this kind of relationship, but the Lord is the one who offers the real unity.

Now as I continue to share with you my story, I must tell you that remembering what happened brings tears to my eyes that I do not have the power to stop, so deep is the anguish in my memory. It is as though my heart is being sliced with a knife each time I recall how I watched the front yard of the church turned into white like snow, as our church was attacked by Muslim neighbors and were ripped out our Bible from Genesis through Revelation and thrown to the ground. The covers of the New Testament and the Old Testament were thrown into a sewer that was in front of the church. The church building itself which had just been completed through hard work and prayer and fasting, was also destroyed.

Each time December approaches, my heart breaks and tears fill my eyes. I remember the humiliation and mockery and my inability to reply to such violence that destroyed the dignity and pride of the Christian people I served. I have always felt proud of my Christian faith and expressed this by placing the bible itself in a special place. The tearing of the Bible pages in front of me and the people I served, tore at my heart. Even more painful was the fact that the security officers whose responsibility it was to protect us, stood idly by with a look in their eyes that said, "Nothing will protect or defend you."

The ache of our hearts was multiplied as we watched our attackers break our musical keyboard into two pieces. The building itself was dismantled, the front being torn down, and three roof tiles removed one by one and thrown until each was broken into pieces. The window glass on the front wall was shattered.

To be honest, I felt as though I was no longer in the country of my birth because there was not compensation or defense, even though I tried to report this violence to the authorities. I was told it was a crowd action and there was nothing that could be done.

We held a Christmas service on December 25TH on the piles of the remaining building of our church. Heavy rains soaked the earth as well as our Christmas outfits, for there was no longer any roof that could protect us from the rain. I personally could not tell if it was the rain or my tears that soaked my outfit. Our singing of Christmas carols like "Silent Night" eased my sadness a bit and lessened the million questions carried by my congregation—"Why is this happening? Where is God?" As a leader I could not answer at the moment because those same questions arose in my own heart. "How could they do this to us? Why would they do this to us?" I realized that life is too short to hold onto my hurt. I had to forgive. I was not the only one that experienced such discrimination. There are still so many events that are more brutal and harder to forgive and certainly hard to forget.

BLEEDING AMBON . . .

I have a sample story taken from the city of Ambon in Indonesia. The name of the event has come to be known as "Bleeding Ambon". This particular story is very impressive as it shares about the courage and obedience of a student in a Sunday school. This student was in a church that was attacked by Muslim rioters. One rioter called this child out in front of his class and ordered him to renounce Jesus. The child refused to renounce Jesus and thus his arms and legs were amputated one by one. The child bled to death, but did not deny Jesus.

It is important to know that "Bleeding Ambon" was not about religion, but more about a certain political agenda that was trying to replace the current president of thirty-three years.

For some time there were those who strategized about this goal of removing the president. The real victim in this matter was religion and how it was used to separate the Indonesian people from each other. A deeper analysis of the situation reveals that there were some who were interested in provoking discord in the country so that the current government would be destabilized. This was done by introducing conflict in the name of religion. This involved spreading lies to Muslims and Christians about each other's religion.

VIOLENCE AGAINST CHINESE . . .

There is another occurrence of violence that may help the reader to understand the situation in Indonesia. It involves the raping of Chinese ethnic women. Due to the success of Chinese ethnics, who are known for their hard work ethic, their "fighting spirit and their "never give up" attitude, a social jealousy developed among other Indonesians. Almost every line of the economy was controlled by Chinese ethnics such that they represented four percent of the total population yet controlled almost 80% of the existing businesses. Even though there was a depressing economic situation at that time, the Chinese ethnics would drive fancy new cars while so many others around them lived under bamboo roofs and some even along the dirty riverside. This practice of flaunting their material success caused a high level of conflict.

Other issues of injustice also existed, such as when a group called Pribumi (local native citizens) worked in similar positions to the Chinese ethnics, the Pribumi would earn 50% less salary than the Chinese ethnic, if they worked in a company run by someone of Chinese descent. Such unfair treatment in business transactions and through racial discrimination created an environment where Chinese ethnics were deemed exclusive or arrogant.

This situation also led to the rape of Chinese-ethnic women that took place in main roads and open space. Stopping cars or motorcycles and public transportation women and girls were kidnapped from their husbands and families. They were stripped of their clothes in public and collectively raped and finally killed.

Another way of attacking was done by breaking into residences and condos and stores and stealing property and raping the women and girls and afterwards killing them. In several locations houses and stores were also burned to the ground.

Such cases are difficult to prove, especially in the case of sexual harassment, because they require facts and evidence that victims feel reluctant to share in public. There were many more issues that triggered the mass rapes such as various issues where business or political competition existed or where there was conflict of interest.

While it is true that 90% of this Chinese ethnic group **are** Christian, and 90% of the Indonesian population is Muslim, the mass rapes were not about religion, but about politics and economics. The primary agenda was to bring down the ruling leader at that time.

INDONESIAN
GOVERNMENT ISSUES . . .

T here is yet more information that the reader must know in order to understand the situation in Indonesia. There was an event widely known as the G30S (committed by the PKI Indonesian Communist Party). In this event, the PKI kidnapped a number of high-ranking Generals, tortured and killed them, and threw seven of their bodies into an alligator's hole (namely lubang buaya). This became a concern of the ruling leader at that time. He set aside September 30th as a special day of commemoration to remember and honor the Pancasila the five commands of Indonesia. Through that event there was a formation of the Left extremist and the Right extremist. The Left wanted to establish a communist country while the Right wanted to build an Islamic country. Both became the enemies of the national government and of the Indonesian people.

From this time forward, Ambon City was divided into two different areas, one for Muslims and one for Christians. If you did not have a religion the government considered you communist.

RELIGIOUS DIVERSIFICATION IN INDONESIA

To understand how Islam became the majority religion in Indonesia, one must go back to the time before Islam came to Indonesia. Before Islam and before Christianity, the primary religions of Indonesia were Buddhist and Hindu. In fact, Indonesians to this day take great pride in the beauty of the Hindu Borobudur temple which is amongt the Seven Wonders of the World. There are even more temples such as Prambanan Temple and Mendut Temple, which are popularly known in the international community. In addition, Bali City, is very well known beyond the borders of Indonesia. An understanding of Indonesia must include an appreciation of the natural wonders of the country. The most beautiful sea park in the world namely Bunaken in North Sulawesi in the city of Manado must be visited so that one can witness the glory of Indonesia's natural beauty and also experience the peaceful relationship which people of Muslim and Christian faith carry for each other. In fact, Manado, in North Sulawesi is known as the city of smiling faces. It is the birth place of my two parents,

Timbuleng-Sumolang. The friendliness of its population can be sensed by observing the harmony between different religious groups. For example, Christian people can build a church with the assistance of Muslims, and Muslims can build a Mosque with the assistance of Christians. Though outsiders may find it hard to believe, this is the true nature of native Indonesian people who have not been contaminated by the people who want to bring the current government down, and thus create a government of the ruling elite based on self-interest and not the interests of the wider population.

The presence of Borobudur Temple reminds one that the main religions of ancient Indonesia were Hindu and Buddhist. There were also animists and atheists. One must also remember that the culture of Indonesia was shaped by people from different countries including India, China, and Arabia. This gave rise to such communities that later came to be known as Arab Village and Chinatown. The Indian influence can be most easily seen through work of the movie production company and school in Pasar Baru.

The Dutch arrived and ruled Indonesia for a very long period of 350 years, followed by the Japanese occupation that lasted three and a half years. The Indonesian hatred towards Christianity was due to the occupation and subjugation by the Dutch who in the name of Christianity oppressed the Indonesian people for 350 years. In the name of Christianity, the Dutch spoke of love and compassion, but actually practiced colonialism and forced labor. A deeper discussion of this will follow in a later chapter.

Another hatred developed against the Chinese, many of whom were landlords who coerced Indonesians to sell their rice fields at a low price. Those who resisted selling their land to the Chinese were killed. Additionally, the Chinese committed terrible acts of violence in the city streets. All of these started a root of hatred toward the Chinese that was passed from generation to generation.

MUSLIMS ARRIVE IN
INDONESIA . . . .

I t is because of this history with the Dutch and the Chinese, that Christians and Chinese came to be hated in Indonesia. This situation created an opening for Islamic people to come into Indonesia's coastal area and unite the Indonesian nation by dealing with the injustice caused by the Dutch Christians and the abusive treatment from *babah ong* or Chinese ethnics. Islam spread over all of Indonesia.

THE INDONESIAN GOVERNMENT

O n August 17, 1945, Indonesia was freed from the colonialism of the Dutch and the Japanese. In 1945 a five point Pancasila (decree) was enacted. The first point of the decree called for belief in God and a clause require Sharia law to be obeyed. This rule calling on people to follow Sharia law was rejected after only a few months. However, in 1966 a group called the "Sixty-Sixers" came into power and developed a new Pancasila (decree), respecting other religions by defending a country under the umbrella of belief in one supreme God. This meant all citizens were free to choose and believe in any religion. The only thing that was prohibited was having no religion or being communist. This meant that the Islamic undertones of the 1945 Pancasila were removed.

INDONESIA AND THE
GLOBAL ECONOMY

An important economic turning point for Indonesia (one might say the point of no return) had to do with whether Indonesia was going to remain prosperous but isolated from the rest of the world, or whether it would choose to engage the global economy.

The decision to engage the global economy created a separation of economic class in Indonesia such that some became very wealthy and many became very poor. Some had the means and the desire to invest large sums of money in risky ventures. However, not everyone could do this. Hence an inequality of opportunity emerged. The real opportunities only belonged to those who were very wealthy. This was the beginning of the social gap that happened in the aftermath of colonialism. The thing that separated people was no longer Christianity or being Chinese, but the rather whether one had the ability to invest, and the ability to speak a foreign language and thus engage the global economy with is possibilities for increasing one's wealth.

Private and state-owned enterprise sectors became wealthy while the Cooperative sector did not. Program Bapak Angkat (assistance provided by private and state-owned sectors) was established but there was corruption such that the Cooperative sector did not receive what it was due.

The largest percentage of Indonesians are farmers and cattlemen so the Cooperative sector plays an important role in Indonesia. However, the money that is supposed to support farmers and cattlemen, is often siphoned off by "middle men" who take their cut and reduce the amount of financial support that is due to those working in agriculture (farmers, cattlemen, and those working in fisheries).

The thirty-three year leadership of the New Order which succeeded in defending Indonesia in terms of the freedom to choose religion, namely Islam, Christianity, Buddhism, and Hinduism came to an end in 1998. Up to that time all were protected under a set of applicable laws, that were taken from the Principle Basis, namely the Pancasila, as indicated in its first principle: Belief in one supreme God. It defended this country's belief in God, by prohibiting any communist activities and insisting that each individual name his or her religious preference. Such a glorious achievement deserves high tribute and appreciation.

The leadership of the New Order, despite the fact that there were a lot of weaknesses, generally succeeded in ruling the country of the largest Muslim population, without becoming a Muslim country. During the New Order there were no church burnings, destruction, or significant numbers of cases of rape.

It was provocateurs that brought down the strong and solid New Order government by creating conflicts between religious groups, especially Islamic and Christian. That in the end has made chaos in Indonesia and has led to the raping of Chinese ethnics and also the burning of church buildings.

A BIT OF MY OWN STORY . . . .

I t all started when I studied in a kindergarten with a close friend. Through high school and even now we remain good friends. We even worked together in carrying out a contractor business that took tenders from the DKI government offices. At that time while we worked together, I was already married with three children. Although we lived far from each other I frequently visited his house and stayed over, perhaps because his family considered me as their own son. Through this family the Lord spoke to me verbally. He reminded me that I have had a close Muslim friend for 30 years. My memory of this friend brought tears to my eyes. For thirty years I had eaten at their house, on occasion slept at their house, joined in their picnics, and even built a joint construction business. Only one time in thirty years did the father of my friend ask me about becoming a Muslim. He said to me half-jokingly, "Timbuleng, Islam is the last religion, so why don't' you convert to Islam?" While he was still smiling I told him in a normal tone of voice, "No, Uncle." I cried because in the 30 years of knowing that family, this was the only time

I had ever been asked about converting to Islam. Never had I been mocked or harassed or heard any negative talk about my Christianity. My Islamic friends never spoke ill of my Christian faith, even though they were a respectable and noble family in Indonesian society at the time. One of the members of the family was a four-star general and later became a minister in the government for 25 years. Even though they were Muslim and famous, they did not speak ill of Christianity either in front of me or behind my back.

For some time, the experience of my church being destroyed by a group of Muslims caused me to lump all Muslims together, as extremist terrorists. But then, God opened my memory and my heart. I remembered my Muslim childhood friend and his family and their gracious hospitality towards me, even though they knew I was a Christian. In all that time, I had never experienced any violence or hurt from Muslim people. What I hope the reader will understand is that inter-faith relationships are vital to the health of the whole human family. This means that we must understand the history and nuances of the faith experiences of others. It is vital that we understand that extremism is not the whole story when it comes to Muslims. Quite the opposite, I have been privileged to know Muslims who live lives of love and generosity.

The story I have shared with you is one of my own transformation. The experience of having my church attacked by a crowd of Muslims temporarily closed my heart with anger and bitterness. I wanted revenge. I wanted others to hurt as I had been hurt. But then God reached into my heart and mind and opened me up again. God used my memory of my childhood friendship to fashion a new beginning. I rediscovered a truth I had known from an early age: That not all Muslims are extremists. This rediscovery was a gift from God so that I could move to forgiveness and be free of my anger and bitterness. What I have been trying to clarify with regard to the situation in Indonesia is that not all responsibility for the crime and violence in Indonesia can be blamed on people of the Muslim faith. The history of Indonesia suggests a much more complicated picture in which social and economic gaps were created between the rich and poor. While Muslims have been blamed for this situation, it was often the failure of Christians to tend the needs of the poor that contributed to the environment of conflict.

My hope is that my story will enable others to discover what I have been blessed to rediscover. Islam is not a religion of violence. Though people who claim to be Muslim have engaged in acts of violence, they do not represent the core of Islamic belief. Rather they seek their own ends. Often the pain of 9/11 is still so great, that it is hard to separate an extremist impression of Islam from one that is loving and generous.

My heart aches for the whole human family to discover that God has called us all into relationships of love and justice. This is my core understanding of what it means to be Christian. Regardless of one's faith tradition, I urge those who read this work of mine to share this alternative view of who Muslims are with others.

A CHANGED PERSPECTIVE

My reflections about my past and the history of my native country of Indonesia have brought me to a new discovery. I now realize that I am not alone regarding the deep emotions I feel as I think about my new perspective. I realize that all people suffer because of misunderstanding of each other. The tragic result of this misunderstanding is that armies continue to fight each other presuming that "the other" is always an enemy. In fact this is not the case. Many share the desire that I share to exist in peace based on mutual respect of different faith traditions. Tragically too much money has been spent and too many lives have been lost due to a failure to recognize our common humanity and the truth that God loves everyone.

I have no idea how much American money has been spent on the wars in Afghanistan and Iraq. It seems clear to me that the Lord would say that one million dollars in American money for one missile is too much. What if this same money could be used for helping the victims of natural disasters or subsidizing the economic sector that has been challenged all this time?

It seems that our misunderstandings of each other have multiplied our tragedies, such that our resources of people and money have been misdirected towards death and destruction, instead of growth and reconciliation.

So these important questions have answers: is a Muslim person your enemy? Certainly not. Who is your brother or sister? In Christ, we can recognize that Muslims are our brothers and sisters, as are all members of God's human family.

A CRACKED WALL PORTRAIT
→ THE IMAGE

Introduction

I n the writing of this book, God spoke to me directly through an analogy of a cracked wall portrait which led me to title this book, *The Image*. An analogy regarding what God is doing may be helpful. Imagine a well-behaved girl, who comes from a generous family, regularly practicing her religion. The image of her life may be represented as a wonderful and adorable wall portrait. However, this girl suddenly discovers she is pregnant without being previously married, and even worse, nobody knows who the biological father of her baby is, or who is responsible for her pregnancy. At this point, the wonderful wall portrait is suddenly broken, and a cloudy future emerges for her.

As human beings, we may hope that God would perfectly change the end of the story of that girl by fitting the situation of her pregnancy in the middle of her life, after she has had a chance to marry, so that her life might remain straight and smooth. Yet, there are times when things do not happen according to our best hopes or plans. Still God has a way of fashioning a new future and bringing healing.

There is no surprise for God. The Psalmist reminds us, even in the womb, God knew you (Psalm 139: 13). He is the alpha and omega, the beginning and the end, the author and the completion (Revelation 21:6). The final vision is God's, regardless of what people say or where you were born. God has the very last word. Amen.

The story about the life of Christianity and Islam in Indonesia is closely represented by this analogy (i.e. a cracked wall portrait) and essentially, the ending has the potential to be wonderful. God has a larger vision than that which the devil tempts us to embrace. When human beings embrace this vision of God's ability to bring all people together, the rule of the devil's temptation to separateness loses its power. The happy ending of the story of the human family will lead to the ultimate loss of the kingdom of the devil. On the one hand, no matter how simple or negligible our sins are, they will lead to the loss of God's kingdom. On the other hand, no matter how simple or negligible our generous behaviors, they will lead to the loss of the kingdom of the devil.

We can simply find a good example about this in the daily life of a married couple. A married couple who can understand each other easily shall influence the community and the surrounding area. Therefore they should be a role model for the other families. On the other hand, one ultimate mission of the devil is to breakdown every single good family, so that those families break up and the family members may fall easily into violence, the use of drugs, prostitution, and many other crimes. If one thinks further about the devastation of a marriage, such brokenness started from simple matters, such as egoism, resistance from positive criticism, and many others. So, it seems it has been with Christianity and Islam. The mission of these two religions began in the heart of God, but egoism and failure to listen to each other prevented each from living out their deepest purpose. If we think back to Christianity and Islam, these two religions basically possess the same mission, to reveal the life of God. But because they failed to get along, each blurred the wonderful image they had been shown initially.

What the Bible Says?

A reflection from the Hebrew Testament of the Bible reflects the root of these religions (i.e. Christianity and Islam). The common root of Christianity and Islam is our ancestor Abraham. Abraham had a wife Sarah who was barren. So that Abraham and Sarah could have an heir, Sarah offered her slave Hagar to Abraham so they could have children. Hagar bore a son, Ishmael. Later, God opened the womb of Sarah and she bore a son, Isaac. The root of the differences between these two religions is that Islam claims that Ishmael is the chosen one because he is the first-born to Abraham. Hence, since Ishmael represents the root of Islam. The Hebrew Testament of the Bible tells us that it was Isaac who was offered as a sacrifice to God. My research in fact shows that Abraham offered a lamb instead of any of his sons. Furthermore, one can find the similarity between these two religions through their holy books. For example, the contents of the Psalms from the Heberew Testament of the Christian's Holy Bible are the same as the contents of the book of Zabur in Islam's Holy Qur'an.

The "White Christian and Colonialism in Indonesia

The following thesis explains the background why the Indonesians hate the so-called "white Christian people" by exploring the historical roots of colonialism and the initial spread of Christianity in Indonesia.

Colonialism in Indonesia was started a several centuries ago (approximately in the 15th century) by the arrival of the European traders who sailed far away to look for unique spices that could not be found in their homeland. Traders from Portugal, Spain, England and the Netherlands are among the people who colonialized the Indonesian Isles. Among those nations, The Netherlands took the longest turn by occupying the Indonesian Islands for about 350 years. The Dutch people who initially conducted trading to fulfill their needs of spices and other various natural resources, become the most ruthless colonists in Indonesian history. What is obvious from this phase is that these people colonialized through their armed forces, taking the people's land, and doing many other bad things. On the other hand, they built worship places, conducted Christmas and Easter celebrations, weekend services, Sunday school for kids and spreading out the words about how people should love each other as they love themselves. Those teachings were completely contradictory to their actions. In addition, the behaviors of drunkenness, like a never ending party, abusing young girls, and so many other evil behaviors led to a deep hatred by the Indonesians of the colonists, who unfortunately proclaimed themselves as Christians. This situation had been going on for at least 350 years, therefore it is very understandable that most Indonesians experienced a deep wound in their hearts which fostered this hatred for anyone who claimed themselves to be "white" or Christian. Not only did the colonist become a target of their hatred but also Christianity became a target of their hatred, as well. Further, any Indonesian who turned to Jesus and proclaimed themselves Christian, were labeled a "colonist's bootlicker." This reality opened the door for Islam to be welcomed by the people of Indonesia. It was Muslims who tended the needs of the people and thus became a living witness to the love of God.

The Emergence of Terrorism Within Islam

Many are unfamiliar with this loving witness of Islam. Sadly, the experiences of 9/11, including the death of thousands and the destruction of the World Trade Center towers, have shaped for many a view of what Islamic people are like. Many people came to the inaccurate conclusion that all Muslims are simply terrorists or even further that Islam is a religion of terror. However, one must take a much broader perspective, since none of these actions were suggested or could be implied from the teachings of Mohammed in the Holy Qur'an. The perpetration of all these terrible acts of violence are a worship of violence and have nothing to do with the worship of God as taught by Islam's Holy Qur'an.

Appropriate Point of View

Therefore, in this book, I would like to encourage every reader to step back from their prejudices and assumptions about Islam as a source of terror and evil, and set everything back in in its proper historical and theological perspective.

A Vision of Hope

In contrast to all these religious-rooted conflicts, I would ask the reader to see a different image, a situation where people with different religious views and practices live alongside each other peacefully. There is a city in Indonesia called Manado, which lies in the Province of North Sulawesi. Here, all inhabitants, regardless of their religious views, live peacefully based on the first principle of Indonesia as a nation, which is called Pancasila (or the five nation's principles). The first principle is "Belief in One God". This principle implies that, all citizens shall be tolerant with other fellow citizens in terms of practicing officially acknowledged religions.

There are 6 officially recognized religions in Indonesia based on the renewed constitution of the year 2000, during Abdurrahman Wahid's Presidential Era. They are: Islam, Christian (Protestant, Pentecostal and others), Roman Catholic, Buddhist, Hindu and Confucian. The government protects every citizen who practices one of these religions.

As I mentioned before, in Manado,, the building of a Christian worship place would always get help from Islamic neighbors, and the other way around. There is a great harmony that exists. Further, Manado is famous for the existence of abundant churches in every alley, which stand next to a few mosques.

In other parts of Indonesia, one could easily find a township or even a big city that is dominated by Christians with many places of worship, such as in the most eastern part of Indonesia, North Sumatera. Even in some parts of Central Java, there exists a huge Theological School with many students. There are even some visiting professors from abroad from such places as the United States. To name some more, there are several big theological schools around Jakarta, Indonesia's capital, and in West Java, where the majority of the population is Muslim.

This being said, it seems inappropriate to categorize Indonesia as a fundamentalist Islamic country. Even further, it is inappropriate to blame and target Indonesia as having a major role in the 9/11 tragedy. The actions of a few should not be allowed to obscure how the majority of Muslims in Indonesia think and act.

To present another example of religious tolerance in Indonesia, one may go up to Kalimantan hinterland, where there are a lot of churches built in remote areas, which could not be reached by any vehicle. Also on Java Island, even though the majority of the population is Muslim, one can easily find churches spread out at Java hinterland with mixed-religious communities living together without significant conflict rooted from differences based on religion.

However, if one looks hard enough, one will discover that several Christian worship places have been destroyed by Muslims since 2011. As the reader will remember, such was my experience with the church I served. Yet this represents a very small percentage of the experience of Christians related to Muslims.

Governmental Challenges

Anti-Muslim prejudice has been encouraged by a group which desires to take over the current government engaging in activities that the cause the rest of the world to downgrade its evaluation of the current government's performance. The strategy of this anti-government group consists of a series of violence based religious conflicts such as the recent devastation of Christians churches by a very small minority of Muslims. By introducing this violence, this group hopes the current government will be perceived as weak, due to the failure to overcome these problems. In this way they hope to accomplish their plan to take over the government.

This strategy has worked pretty well in the last few years, since the government indeed failed to enforce the law to overcome the conflicts and their resulting impact.

I, as the author, really hope that the current government could get back to its strong enforcement against violence; thereby minimizing the impact caused by conflicts from different religious practices. I further hope the opportunist group, who is trying to take over the current government, would embrace a healthy competition in pursuing a position in the government of Indonesia, and leave their violent practices in the past.

For my Muslim friends, I beg your understanding about the position of Indonesia among the countries of world, which is significantly important. Therefore, the spread of misleading information about other religions or similar but different religions could be minimized and restore the image of Indonesia as the most tolerant country in the world. Further, this situation could also lead to a wave of tourists who want to enjoy the beauty of Indonesia. Investors may also want to work and directly assist in Indonesia's economic development. My hope is that such investment could help the economic situation of middle and lower class communities in Indonesia to a higher standard of living. Let us hold each other's hands and restore the economy of this country, which used to be very stable and strong.